RUNNING
MARATHONS

IN 50 STATES AND 7 CONTINENTS

A RUNNER'S INSPIRATIONAL ADVENTURE
AROUND THE WORLD

ROBERT PRESTON

ISBN 978-1-63903-811-4 (paperback)
ISBN 978-1-63903-812-1 (digital)

Christian Faith Publishing, Inc.
832 Park Avenue
Meadville, PA 16335
www.christianfaithpublishing.com

Printed in the United States of America

After competing in and most often winning grueling marathons in all 50 states Rob, with a healthy dose of authority, can tell anybody what is so great about Athens, TN. Rob is obviously a very competitive person, and when you are a competitive person, it is a part of your fiber. It drives your thinking and feeds your desires. It directs your actions.

—Peyton Manning (June 27, 2015)

What an American experience. Preston, one of the kindest men I've ever met, has encountered this country in a way most of us never will. It is one thing to tourist-travel through a place, yet quite another to encounter an American state and its people by running 26 miles through it.
He's run through Mississippi heat. Thirty-mile-per-hour headwinds in Texas. Run down old railroad paths in Virginia.
Through the white snow of New England.
Past Lake Mead and Hoover Dam, where the sky and lake were perfect blue.
He ran through the aspens and John-Denver-highs of Colorado. In Alaska, eagles flew nearby.
In Vermont, deer. Bears in Montana, snakes in Iowa, and of course, the most exhilarating crowds, thick as chowder, in Boston.
He's run through asthma attacks, darkness, snowstorms, dehydration.
One race, he almost blacked out.

—David Cook (June 16, 2015),
award-winning journalist
Chattanooga Times Free Press

I am astounded by your running talents, Rob.

—George W. Bush (June 22, 2019, in a personal letter)
43rd President of the United States

Keep Running

Robert Proshu

CONTENTS

INTRODUCTION

I love to run, and my love for running has taken me all around the world. From Boston and New York to Antarctica and South Africa, I have gotten to see some of the most beautiful scenery on the planet. I have run 115 marathons in all fifty states as well as the seven continents. Like all athletes, I have had setbacks. Through faith, perseverance, and determination, I have kept going and learned that the human will is powerful. One of my goals in writing a book is to inspire people to dream big, whether it is running or something else. Do not let anyone, including yourself, say that a goal is impossible or unattainable!

So why should you read this book especially if you are not a runner? The following are ten life lessons I have learned from running, and I have tried to apply all ten to this book with the hope that it can motivate and possibly help you accomplish a goal or get you through a tough situation in life.

- *Do not stop when things get tough*—When we are young, we tend to give up when things around us get hard. Running teaches us that the reward comes when we keep going even though it is difficult. You will read some of the difficult situations I have faced.
- *Achieving your goals takes hard work*—If you want to finish the race, you must put in all the preliminary mileage and training that is needed to get you in top condition. Likewise, if you want to graduate from college or run a successful business, you need to put in the work to accomplish your goal.

- *You are stronger than you think*—With hard work, training, and dedication to your goals, you might surprise yourself with what you can accomplish. It really is amazing what the human body can accomplish and endure. There are several examples in this book of how I had to persevere through extreme adversity.
- *Everything is mental*—Running teaches you that your mind is your best tool. It can get you through those times when you feel like your legs cannot carry you one more step. Like the football kicker who goes out on the field with four seconds left to kick the winning field goal, running is mental. Of course, one must be in good shape to run a marathon, but the bigger challenge is believing that you can do it.
- *You do have the time*—If you want something badly enough, you will find the time. I get up every morning before three. Some mornings, I don't feel like it, but I get up anyway because I want to be the best I can be. This also applies to my spiritual life—before I walk out the door for a run, I have a morning devotion and prayer time. I want to do those things first before my workday gets started.
- *You can do hard things*—Life is hard. Running teaches you that you can do hard things. Whether it is running a marathon, acing that job interview, or raising a family, you have got this.
- *You define you*—You get to choose the runner or person you want to be. Not your parents, your teachers, your friends, your spouse, not even your coach. You can choose to push yourself to a higher level, stay where you are, or somewhere in between depending upon your goals and the effort you expend. This is one of the things I love about running. Like tennis and basketball, I do not need others to *participate with*. I can go out at 2 a.m. and be alone for three hours enjoying the moon and stars.
- *There are no shortcuts, hacks, or tricks*—To succeed in running or life, you must put in the work. It is as simple as that. I have sometimes been described as *too nice*. That

might be true, but I am extremely competitive, and I know that to be my best at running or anything, I have got to put the time in to be successful.

- *Just because you make mistakes, learn from them, and keep going*—I have made plenty of mistakes in running as well as in life. I have even devoted an entire chapter to learning from mistakes. The issue is not making a mistake because we all make them. The bigger issue is learning from them and making yourself stronger.
- *It is a marathon, not a sprint*—We have all heard this expression before, but it is so true in a race as well as in life.

1

THE ADVENTURE STARTS

As I boarded the plane to Antarctica, my excitement and adrenaline were off the charts. Sitting on the plane for the short, two-hour flight from Punta Arenas, South America, I couldn't help but think about what brought me to this point.

Growing up, I always played sports like basketball, baseball, and tennis, but running was always a part I didn't enjoy. In junior high basketball, running was a punishment for me if the team missed free throws or didn't execute a play correctly.

Later, when I "walked on" the East Tennessee State University tennis team and during my freshman year, one of my teammates got caught buying beer in the grocery store by, of all people, the coach. As a punishment, the entire team had to get up early for a month and run sprints.

I had a wonderful childhood. My brother Mark and I have a great friendship as well as a love for sports. We would literally get involved in any game we could find and sometimes, we would even make up games. Basketball was our favorite sport to play, and we had numerous games in the driveway, and during the weekends, we would find pickup games at the community gym up the street. Once we got old enough to drive, we would go to the UTC (University of Tennessee Chattanooga) gym with three friends for pickup games. Those evenings were priceless as we would walk in the gym, and no one took us seriously. But once it was our turn to play, we very rarely lost. It was a lot like Billy Hoyle (Woody Harrelson) in the movie *White Men Can't Jump*. None of us could jump or was really fast or flashy, but we could play team ball as well as anyone, and while the opponent would eventually figure it out, it usually was too late as we were way ahead.

Attending college at East Tennessee State University was a wonderful experience. My brother Mark was already there when I started as a freshman. My grandparents lived in Johnson City, so every weekend, Mark and I stayed with them. There are so many wonderful memories of eating together (my grandmother was a great cook), attending church, plus hours and hours of Gin Rummy. College is also where I met my wife, Sarah. It was fun going on dates and to ballgames with her as well as going to her parents' house in Elizabethton, a few miles away. Like my grandmother, Sarah's mother is also a wonderful cook. (You can see a theme developing—how much I love good food!)

During my freshman year, I made the ETSU tennis team. It was a valuable experience as far as developing discipline and hard work in me. I was not the most talented and maybe the least talented of anyone on the team. However, I had a work ethic that made me competitive on the college level. I believe that first year really helped develop me into a good student. I learned the key was studying each day and not waiting until the night before like some students. I guess it is like training for a marathon—I train each day to prepare for the test or race.

After college, I continued to play pickup basketball games as well as tennis anytime I could find someone with whom to play. Those sports faded away mainly because it was hard to do them on my schedule. I needed something that I could do by myself and still be competitive.

My running adventures started in November of 1997 when my good friend and former college roommate, Bob Avento, asked me to participate with him in the New York City Marathon. At that time, I had never run more than a 5K. I had played high school basketball and tennis and always run to stay in shape, but when the opportunity arose, I felt both excited and nervous about running 26.2 miles. Over the next eight months, I began to realize how much I loved to run and pushed myself beyond what I thought I could do. Even still, I was not completely sure how much I would enjoy that marathon, as well as the travel experience. Growing up in Tennessee, I had flown only a few times before and never to a big city.

Hopefully, there will be nonrunners who will read this book, and some might wonder about the history of the marathon. So I thought it would be good to explain a little about how the marathon got started and why it is 26.2 miles.

The marathon may have ancient roots, but the footrace's official length of 26.2 miles was not established until the twentieth century. The first organized marathon was held in Athens at the 1896 Olympics, the start of the Games' modern era. The ancient games, which took place in Greece from around 776 BC to AD 393, never included such long-distance races. The idea for the modern marathon was inspired by the legend of an ancient Greek messenger who raced from the site of Marathon to Athens, about forty kilometers, or nearly twenty-five miles, with the news of an important Greek victory over an invading army of Persians in 490 BC. After making his announcement, the exhausted messenger collapsed and died. To commemorate his dramatic run, the distance of the 1896 Olympic marathon was set at forty kilometers.

For the next few Olympics, the length of the marathon remained close to twenty-five miles, but at the 1908 Games in London, the course was extended, allegedly to accommodate the British royal family. As the story goes, Queen Alexandra requested that the race start on the lawn of Windsor Castle and finish in front of the royal box at the Olympic stadium—a distance that happened to be 26.2 miles (26 miles and 385 yards). The random boost in mileage ended up sticking, and in 1921, the length for a marathon was formally standardized at 26.2 miles (42.195 kilometers).

Today, marathon races take place everywhere from the North Pole to the Great Wall of China. In America alone, there are now more than 1,100 marathons each year. For decades, marathons were only open to male athletes. The Boston Marathon, which kicked off in 1897 and is the world's oldest annual marathon, began allowing female competitors in 1972, while the first Olympic marathon for women was not held until 1984. In 1976, an estimated twenty-five thousand runners finished marathons in the United States; by 2020, the estimated number of competitors who completed a 26.2-mile course had soared to 1,298,725, with an average finish time of 4:29:53. (Information from History.com.)

November arrived, and I was ready and excited. We flew to New York two days before the race and stayed with Bob's grandmother as well as his aunt Grace and her husband Glen. The basement we slept in while there was used by Bob's dad and the band he was in several years ago. A few of the band members included actor Joe Pesci and singer Frankie Valli!

Riding in a car in New York City for the first time was quite an experience. I remember going through a yellow/red light and wondering, *What are we doing?* Then I looked back and saw three cars behind us and realized that if we had stopped, we would have been hit. I was very thankful at that point that someone else was driving!

The day before the race, Bob and I decided to do a little sightseeing. What started out as a *little* turned out to be an all-day excursion. When we were ready to return to Bob's grandmother's, we were supposed to call Glen. Unfortunately, we had written down the wrong area code which led to our all-day visit to New York City. When I went to bed that night, I thought we had been on our feet too much and that it could affect the race the next morning. However, with adrenaline and a good breakfast (lots of bagels and bananas), we were ready to go.

The New York City Marathon is a wonderful event but involves a lot of people. Runners are placed in the starting corrals in order of their projected race time. Having never run a marathon before, Bob and I had no projected time so were placed at the very back of the thirty-five thousand runners. It took twenty-one minutes just to cross the start line! It was probably somewhere around mile 10 that I was able to run at a decent pace. The first ten miles I was forced to run at a slow pace, weaving in and out of the huge crowd. The marathon finished at Central Park, a great way to end the race. My time that day was three hours and forty minutes (5,247th place out of thirty-two thousand). I was happy to have finished, but in the back of my mind wondered how much better I could have done if the crowd had not been so large.

The New York adventure was not quite over as we got ready to head back to Tennessee. We had to hustle to get to our plane. Neither of us had time to shower, so we basically boarded the plane with what we had run in, along with our medals hanging around our necks. I remember the passengers applauding as we entered the cabin. That applause changed a little while later. As it turned out, President Clinton was at the airport, and our plane along with several others was waiting for Air Force One to take off. After sitting in sweaty clothes for an hour, we were not booed, but the other passengers were not exactly thrilled with the odor. We missed our connecting flight in Charlotte, so we were one day later getting home.

With my good friend, Bob Avento, before the New York City Marathon.

It did not take long for me to start thinking about another race. For the next several years, I ran marathons mostly within driving distance, averaging around three or four each year. My confidence grew as my times continued to improve. I averaged around two hours and forty-five minutes and finally broke two hours and forty minutes at the Rocket City Marathon (Huntsville, Alabama) in December of 2002 with a time of two hours and thirty-nine minutes. In 2003, I posted my personal best in the Louisville (Kentucky) Marathon with a time of two hours and thirty-seven minutes.

My first sub-two-hour-and-forty-minute
marathon in Huntsville, Alabama.

2

LEARNING FROM MISTAKES

My successes have not come without mistakes. I am okay with making mistakes as long as I learn from them. One example occurred in September of 2008 when I traveled to Tupelo, Mississippi for the Tupelo Marathon. The start time for the race was early in the morning but that did not stop it from being extremely humid. My first hint that it was going to be a tough race was the race T-shirt design. It was a skull and crossbones, and the skull was sweating blood!

The race started out great. I felt so much energy and ran ahead with a sizeable lead. About halfway through the race, the *bottom fell out*, and the heat started to get to me. My lead was shrinking, and I could hear footsteps behind me. Finally, two runners caught me and then two more, until finally, I crossed the finish line in sixth place. My mistake was running too hard at the beginning and not taking the heat seriously. I probably did not drink enough as well. You should aim to take in six to ten ounces of fluid every two to three miles. If it is a hot day like it was, you should take in a bit more.

There was something about the Tupelo race that I liked and found challenging. I have run it three more times with improvement but still, find it exceedingly difficult. One of those times, my brother Mark and my wife Sarah traveled with me. I ran a good race, but with a few miles left, the heat once again got to me. I remember crossing the finish line, sitting down, and then Mark slapping me on the face trying to keep me from passing out. What a loving brother will do to keep me conscious!

As a marathon runner, one of my biggest nightmares is making a wrong turn during a race. Before 2014, I was fortunate that it had only happened once and was not too much out of the way. I was running in Georgia, and the volunteer at the turn stepped away for only a few seconds, but that was all it took for me to keep running when I was supposed to turn. She jumped into her golf cart and caught me and offered to give me a ride back to the turn. I declined her offer, and I turned and quickly got back to the turn.

Fast forward eight years, and there I was running a strong race in New Hampshire. Another runner and I were far out in front and were enjoying each other's company. I could tell that he was very experienced as well as competitive. Part of the course was through a wooded area. Race instructions had stated that a white marking indicated a turn. So when we came across a white cloth or ribbon tied around a small tree, we turned. We were about 0.9 miles past the turn when both of us, almost at the same time, said, "Oh, no!" We knew we had made a wrong turn. (Later, the race director said the white markings were all spray-painted on the ground and that we should have ignored the tree.)

I guess being a little angry, along with the added adrenaline, made us run extremely hard back to where we had made the wrong turn. This was about halfway through the race. My new friend told me he was thinking about withdrawing since he had another race the following weekend which was evidently more important to him. He kept running for another mile, wished me well, and stopped running. One of the volunteers at the next water stop told me that I was still in first place, but the gap had closed. Telling me things like that is always good and motivated me to keep my pace until the end.

I remember that fateful morning for another reason. About three miles before the finish, I fell trying to hop over a ditch in the woods. It was slick, so I fell. Luckily, I did not get hurt, though I did get extremely muddy. As I approached the finish line, I felt great coming in first, especially after running more like twenty-eight miles than 26.2!

In October of 2006, Bob and I traveled to Washington, DC for the Marine Corps Marathon. A few days before the race, I started feeling sick with a cold. As race day approached, my cold developed into bronchitis. I knew before the race started that it was a mistake to attempt it, but I was there and paid my registration fee, so I was determined to finish the race. At mile 6, breathing was difficult, so I stopped at an aid station where an ambulance was parked. The two nice paramedics were incredibly good to me though one really wanted me to visit the nearby hospital. I pleaded my case, and the other paramedic understood how much I wanted to keep going. They gave me what was equivalent to two breathing treatments of steroids and made me promise to take it slow. After spending almost an hour in the back of the ambulance, I was now back out on the road. The steroids gave me instant relief and little problems for the last three-fourths of the race, though I was sick the two weeks following the race.

After races like those mentioned above, it normally takes a few days for me to get remotivated. But failing, or not doing as well as I would have liked, is a definite motivator for me to keep going and to try harder. Of the 115 marathons I have run, some have gone well, and some have not, but I am proud that I persevered in each one to cross the finish line.

In dealing with how to handle mistakes, one of my favorite coaches is Nick Saban. He spoke at our Chamber of Commerce dinner in 2013 and was a wonderful speaker. Coach Saban is incredibly detailed and disciplined in coaching and in probably everything he does. He has many great motivational quotes, but one I really like is this: "What happened yesterday is history. What happens tomorrow is a mystery. What we do today makes a difference."

Something that has always helped me in my running and in my life is to take one day at a time. I try not to let what happened yesterday, like struggling in a race, get me down. Also, I try not to get so satisfied with what I have accomplished that I am not hungry to do more.

Matthew 6:34 NIV states, "Therefore do not worry about tomorrow, for tomorrow will worry about itself. Each day has enough trouble of its own." As a Christian, it is so comforting to know that I only have to live one day at a time. When tomorrow gets here, God will meet me in the morning and lead me through the day—PRAISE JESUS!

Coach Saban spoke at our chamber dinner in 2013.

3

PIZZA AND SKUNKS

A lot of people ask me how I train and what I eat. I have never had any formal coaching but have read a lot on the Internet and in books. Generally, my training regimen includes seventy miles per week. I have gone over that amount occasionally, but seventy is the average. My long run has always been Monday morning and includes twenty miles. I have set my alarm for over twenty years, and it never goes off. I get up around 1:30 a.m. ready to run. I figure I am either gifted with a built-in alarm or else I have a problem. My guess is it is a little of both.

Before heading outside, I always have devotional time to get my mind and my heart right before running twenty miles. My walk with the Lord is important to me, and I will continue to share more about that throughout this book. I love the early morning hours with the stars and moon shining brightly. Occasionally, someone coming home from work will yell at me. Some of the comments would not be appropriate for this book, but I have heard the "Run, Forrest, run" phrase multiple times.

Because I am running in the dark, I also see a lot of animals including dogs, cats, deer, opossums, snakes, and yes, skunks. Needless to say, I have come very close to an unkind encounter with a skunk. Fortunately, so far, they appear just as afraid of me as I am of them.

My wife, Sarah, has been very supportive since we've been married. She has been very patient with my unusual sleep schedule and training regimen. She is a wonderful schoolteacher and wakes up around six each morning. With me running so early, I can come back and see her before she goes off to school. It is a blessing to call her my wife and best friend.

I have found that each day of the week is especially important to my training schedule. After the long run on Monday morning, I try to do something that afternoon just to keep my legs fresh, maybe a light jog on the track or treadmill. Tuesday is a shorter run of only five miles, but equally important. As hard as it is sometimes to get out of bed after a grueling day on Monday, I try to run the five miles at a good pace. That technique seems to set up positively the rest of the week. Wednesday's training consists of a thirteen-mile run followed by Thursday, an important day in which I do speed/interval training. Over the years, I have done some of those runs on treadmills but mostly outside on a track. I do a series of laps, alternating between sprinting and jogging, building up to a one-mile sprint. That workout seems to work for me and has been extremely important for me over the years.

Friday is usually another long run of at least fifteen miles. I try to run in a different direction than the Monday run just to change it up some. Some Friday afternoons, I will head to the gym and do a short run on the treadmill. I try hard to sleep a little later on Saturdays, and usually, I can make it till 5:00 a.m. (late for me); and then I usually run nine or ten miles. As with most runners, I am very disciplined and routine-oriented, almost to the point where I am very predictable.

Eating is no different. Being around 155 pounds and running as much as I do, eating is important to me, and as I have already stated, something that I really enjoy. Of course, I do not look like it, but I do eat a lot. Frequently, normally the night before the race, I will visit a local pizza place and order the biggest pizza they have, sometimes sixteen inches in diameter. I like veggies, and usually, I order pizza with no cheese. As the server brings it to me, I see the look on her face as if she is thinking, *There's no way he can eat all this pizza.* About halfway through, the server normally comes back out and asks if I would like a takeout box, and I politely respond, "I think I'll work on it a little more."

I know that I will eat every bite, but it is fun to see the expression when he or she returns to find it gone. More than once, the server has brought people from the kitchen to look at this skinny guy who ate a sixteen-inch pizza. I am certain I have eaten a pizza in all fifty states!

Registered dietitian and author of *Sports Nutrition for Endurance Athletes* Monique Ryan recommends that a marathon runner should eat about four grams of carbs for every pound of body weight. For example, a one hundred fifty-pound runner should consume six hundred grams (two thousand four hundred calories) of carbs per day. I have never been one to measure the grams I consume each day, but those numbers are probably pretty accurate for me.

My breakfast includes fruit, such as blueberries, a peach, or a banana, on a few bowls of cereal. I like shredded wheat or raisin brand but sometimes have other kinds. I also eat two eggs and a bagel or English muffin. To drink, I like chocolate milk, Gatorade, or fresh water.

The job as president of the chamber often involves lunch meetings, and I try to eat as healthy as possible. I have discovered that the more I eat for lunch, the sleepier I get in the afternoon, so I usually do not eat heavily because I want to be good and alert at my job. When I do not have a lunch meeting, I will go home to eat. After I feed our son (Teddy, our cat), I usually will have a large sweet potato and peanut butter on crackers or pretzels. For dessert, I may eat a granola bar or a bowl of oatmeal with raisins.

After getting home from work, I prepare my dinner which is the largest meal of the day. This is when I normally load up on carbs. I will eat a piece of grilled chicken or salmon on pasta or rice. I also like to make my own pizza from premade crust bought at the grocery store. I always include a bagel and green salad with my dinner. Sarah has many gifted traits, and one is being a great shopper! She buys meals that come in bags and normally, it will feed a family of four or six which is perfect for me. The bag might have chicken or shrimp with vegetables and pasta.

Before bedtime, I like to have a nice-sized bowl of fruit. It will include an apple, grapes, bananas, and whatever else is in season.

4

TRAINING ADVENTURES

It is interesting what can happen between the hours of 2 a.m. and 5 a.m. Since 1998, I have been getting up that early to run. I try to run alternate routes, especially on Mondays when I do twenty miles. One Monday I decided to run down Highway 11 and then three miles out to the interstate and back the way I came. When I got to the interstate and started running back toward Highway 11, I ran into three large dogs. I guess they did not hear me initially, but they were upset after seeing me and were not going to let me pass. At that point, I had two choices: I could wait a little while and hope the dogs went back to their homes, or I could go back toward the interstate and up the ramp onto I-75. It was around 3:20 a.m., and I took option two.

As I got onto the interstate, my pace really picked up. I knew it was around four and a half miles to the next exit. At that time of the morning, it was basically large trucks on the road, and I am sure every driver that I passed thought I was crazy. If I'm honest, I might have to agree. It was almost like crossing a finish line when I got to the next exit and started off the interstate. I promised myself I would never do that again!

Another Monday morning, I had run about 19.5 miles and was close to the house when I tripped and fell on my knee. It was one of those things that happened so fast; before I knew it, I was on the ground. A little disoriented, I walked home and woke up Sarah to tell her I was headed to the emergency room. I was extremely fortunate that even though I needed ten stitches, my kneecap was in good shape. This was the first time in my life that I needed stitches, which was a blessing.

During the early morning hours, I have seen just about everything. Police officers have stopped me to make sure everything was okay. One morning, I noticed several officers riding around, and after about an hour, one pulled over and told me an inmate had escaped and cautioned me to be careful. Fortunately, I never encountered the inmate, but I ran extra hard that morning.

It is quite common as I am running to hear a dog barking. I have learned that usually, the smaller dogs are more of a problem than the larger ones. Do not get me wrong; I love dogs and would never hurt one. One morning as I was running around 3:30 a.m., a small dog charged at me, and I kept running probably at a faster rate. It caught me and bit me on the leg, breaking the skin. With it being only a few miles from my house, I found the phone number when I got home and called the owner. A nice lady answered and told me the dog was up-to-date on his shots. The dog's name was Nipper. She told me the next time I ran by to just call the dog by his name, which is what I did, and we became friends.

5

BOSTON

For a runner, it does not get much better than the Boston Marathon. It is the only marathon in the United States for which you must qualify. I got to participate in both the 1999 and 2000 races. Both years were incredibly special because family members got to be there. At the time, my cousin Carolyn and her husband Bob lived in Gloucester, Massachusetts, which is not far from Boston. They lived in the house that the script for the original stage version of *The Sound of Music* was written, and it was a wonderful treat to spend several days there. Bob and Carolyn were familiar with the race route, so I got to see my family several times along the way.

The Boston Marathon is always held on Patriots' Day, the third Monday of April. Begun in 1897, the event was inspired by the success of the first marathon competition in the 1896 Summer Olympics. The Boston Marathon is the world's oldest annual marathon and ranks as one of the world's best-known road racing events. Its course runs from Hopkinton in southern Middlesex County to Copley Square in Boston. The event attracts five hundred thousand spectators each year, making it New England's most widely viewed sporting event. Though starting with fifteen participants in 1897, the event now attracts an average of about thirty thousand registered participants each year (Wikipedia—Boston Marathon).

The race starts in Hopkinton, which is a small town like Athens where I live (around fourteen thousand people). Unlike my New York Marathon experience, I had a previous marathon qualifying time (two hours and forty-two minutes) to put me near the front.

It was a thrill to stand there listening to the national anthem right before the race. As it started, I felt great and enjoyed every bit of it. About halfway through the race, we passed Wellesley College, an all-women's school. It was fun hearing thousands of girls cheer for us. The timing was good with it being around mile 13, near the halfway point.

Whether you are a Boston Marathon first-timer or a seasoned vet, you have probably heard the horror stories about Heartbreak Hill, the steep, half-mile incline at mile 20 in the race. Perhaps the most notorious of all elevation changes in major marathons, the hill gets its name from the 1936 Boston, in which Johnny Kelly famously patted Ellison Brown on the back as he passed him just before Heartbreak. As the story goes, Brown—the eventual race winner—used the gesture to fuel his competitive fire, ultimately surging ahead of Kelly on the hill and breaking his competitor's heart (Wikipedia). For me, the hill was difficult, but the spectators in the crowd ringing cowbells represented the worst part. I think the purpose of the ringing was to encourage the runners, but at mile 20, I did not want to hear it.

The finish of the race was magical, making a final left turn onto Boylston Street. As I made the turn, there were thousands of people lined up cheering, and it was a wonderful feeling. My time the first year was two hours and forty-seven minutes, and I improved the next year with a two-hour-and-forty-three-minute race. All in all, both years remain wonderful memories.

Feeling good at mile 15.

Finish at Boston.

My wonderful support team. From left to right, Linda
Hurt, Bob Stewart, Bob Barnes, Laura Barnes, Steger
Preston, Mark Preston, and Carolyn Stewart.

6

ALOHA

After running the same regional marathons multiple times, I decided to branch out a little...well, I guess a lot. In September of 2009, I flew to Hawaii to participate in the Maui Marathon. My optimal perfect temperature in which to run would be twenty-five to thirty degrees Fahrenheit with no wind. So as beautiful as Hawaii was, it was too hot and humid for my liking. The race started in the dark, running mainly on flat roads. I felt good and strong for the first half of the race. Then the sun came out as we headed up a large hill. The last four or five miles were a struggle, but I finished in three hours and eleven minutes. After crossing the finish line, I looked toward the medical tent, and it looked like a war zone. I guess I was not the only one who had struggled with the heat that day.

The next day, I went on a tropical rain forest hike showcasing five different waterfalls. One great thing about that experience was getting into the cool water; it felt so good on my sore legs. Another great memory revolves around the wonderful pineapple and fresh fruit we ate. I had eaten pineapple before but not like that! Our tour guide had several large tubs in the back of the van, and all he had to say was, "Help yourself."

It seems like every ten yards, he would stop and shake a tree, and a different exotic fruit would fall. He picked it up, and we got to sample. I love fruit, so that was a great part of the excursion. It was a great day mirroring the entire trip.

It was a long plane ride home that I thought about the race and about possibly running marathons in all fifty states. After all, if I could travel to Hawaii, the rest of the states would involve a shorter plane ride for sure.

7

Touring the USA

The year 2010, at age 40, was one of my best years running. I raced in seven different states, setting course records in four of the seven marathons.

One of those races was Bear Lake, Idaho, a breathtaking place. However, one thing I remember about that race involved a huge hailstorm the day before. Although hail is not unusual, this was golf ball-sized. It did not last long, but my rental car did not appreciate it! Fortunately, my automobile insurance took care of the damage.

During that year, I also visited Gunnison, Colorado, one of the most beautiful places I have visited in the United States. From the airport in Denver, it was a four-hour drive to Gunnison but took much longer because I kept stopping the car to take pictures of the incredible views. I will always remember the golden aspen trees, beautiful creeks, and lakes along with the crispest blue sky I've ever seen.

The Colorado race was a nice course beginning with a descent. Getting used to the altitude was not easy; it probably took the first eight miles to get my breathing under control. I finished with a time of two hours and fifty-eight minutes, good for first place.

Colorado.

The last race of 2010 took place in Booneville, Arkansas. It was an *out and back*, mainly on a highway. Unfortunately for the drivers, the highway was not closed, so there was a huge line of cars and trucks behind us. Only every few miles were the automobiles able to pass, so I was extremely impressed with the cheers and kind remarks from those who had to be patient driving down the highway behind us.

I visited seven more states in 2011 and got to experience more American beauty. One of those races in North Bend, Washington, the Light at the End of the Tunnel Marathon, was aptly named. The race began with an almost three-mile segment through a train tunnel. The race instructions had indicated the need for runners to bring a light. Unfortunately, the light often made things worse. There was moisture in the tunnel which made the light a dull blur. Luckily for me, I had read some of the comments from runners in previous years. A good tip shared for running in a dark tunnel was this: if one feels himself going down a slope, one should move back to the middle. I guess it was one of those mental challenges. As the light got bigger,

I knew I was close to the end of the tunnel. As I emerged from the tunnel, it was a great feeling! The remaining part of the course was beautiful, and it was basically downhill, which was nice.

Coming out of a nearly three-mile-long dark tunnel in Washington.

Running marathons involves overcoming a great deal of adversity both before and during races, and my trip to Texas is a great example. For the last several years, I have battled seasonal asthma. Whenever I get a cold, I suffer from breathing problems. I knew I was in trouble before this race when I looked at the forecast predicting heavy winds. As the race in Abilene started, I faced a strong thirty-mile-per-hour headwind. I remember feeling helpless; it seemed like I was barely moving. This challenge went on mile after mile, but I kept telling myself to keep going. I knew we would eventually make a turn and head in the reverse direction with the wind at our back.

About mile 9, it happened, and it was like a rocket went off inside me. At that point, I was only in sixth place, but I was *flying* and feeling great. Around mile 22, I passed the guy in the lead and ran to the end, finishing in first. It remains one of my greatest accomplishments; not the actual winning of the race but overcoming extreme conditions, not stopping, and finishing strong. I did have to have medical attention after the race and was sick for a week, but it was worth it!

In 2012, I visited nine more states, including the Madison Marathon in Ennis, Montana. This race unfolds along a point-to-point course that averages over nine thousand feet above sea level throughout most of the route and features some of the most spectacular natural beauty in the western United States. The race organizers and sponsors say that this race is the nation's highest elevated marathon road race, and perhaps is the highest of its kind anywhere in the world. This was another race that held spectacular beauty. Wildlife was abundant, including a small black bear. I am sure Mama wasn't too far away, so I kept running.

Madison Marathon, the highest altitude marathon in the United States.

The next race that year was just as beautiful in Price, Utah with the name The Little Grand Canyon Marathon. The first part of the race was mostly on a gravel road, and as we ran, I could see the beauty that was approaching. The second half of the course was spectacular, running through the canyon area and past the ancient Native American wall paintings.

Utah—Little Grand Canyon Marathon.

That year was also memorable because I ran over a snake during the Marathon to Marathon in Iowa. When most people say they ran over a snake, they are most likely referring to driving in a car. In my case, I was running on the shoulder of the highway. I was feeling good and running hard and did not notice until I was a few feet away from it that it was a nice-sized snake. It was alive but did not move; needless to say, I did the moving and ran even harder!

For the next two years, I visited several more states including Alaska. The Alaskan race was held in an interesting town called Cordova. I first flew into Anchorage and from there traveled to Cordova. Evidently, several years ago, an earthquake destroyed the bridge necessary for travel by car, so the only way to reach Cordova is by plane. Strangely, the huge plane I flew to Anchorage was the same plane I flew to Cordova. The airplane was actually larger than the airport. I loved Cordova, and the people were very friendly. After the race, we enjoyed a delicious all-you-can-eat salmon cookout. I also saw three huge eagles while I was there.

By the end of 2014, I was getting awfully close to reaching my goal of running in all fifty states. As I crossed off states 47, 48, and 49, only Vermont remained. On March 28 in Windsor, Vermont, I crossed the finish line and finally achieved my goal of running a marathon in every state. That race was memorable for several reasons; one involves having to run in a driving snowstorm. The snow was beautiful but made running a little difficult, especially on a few of the downhill sections.

I particularly remember the drive back to the Boston airport. As I have mentioned earlier, I'm from a small town, and driving in large cities makes me nervous. Add to that the sideways-blowing snow, and I was thrilled to get to the airport. My wife and I had planned a trip to Florida departing the next day, so I arrived home that night only to drive ten hours to Florida the next morning. For me, it was a lot like when a sports team wins a championship and then goes on vacation to Disney World. The next week was so nice, spending time with Sarah and relaxing on the beach.

Number 50 in Vermont.

8

Running with Poison Ivy

In late May of 2015, I traveled to Winston Salem, North Carolina for the Indoor Insanity Marathon. Some people think that running on a flat surface with a climate-controlled environment would be easier than traditional road or trail running. However, making hundreds of turns is not the best thing for one's knees. Even though this race zigzagged left and right in the infield of the track, it was still eighty-four times around the track. I really did not need or ask for any other challenges with this race, but unfortunately, it came in the form of poison ivy!

I worked in our yard at home the week before the race. The area that I was working on was not covered with poison ivy, but as I've experienced throughout my life, there only needs to be a little, and I will get it. By midweek, I had the red, itchy bumps on my arms and legs. Fortunately, my training was in the tapering mode with not a lot of miles run. Even so, a four- or five-mile run in the humid weather was no fun.

With the race approaching, only a few of the bumps had improved, and I was still uncomfortable. I made the five-hour drive to Winston Salem, and after checking into my hotel, I went to get my race packet. As I approached the table, one of the volunteers took a good look at my arms and she simply said, "I'm sorry." She shared a similar story with me about participating in a trail race with poison ivy everywhere. We then got a good laugh out of it stating what we go through because we love running. I thanked her and headed back to my car.

I did pretty well in the race, and my theory is I probably ran extra hard so it would be over quicker! My time was three hours five minutes, good enough for first place.

9

FANTASTIC FINISHES

As grueling as marathons can be, sometimes motivation to continue lies within an unforgettable finish. I have had the privilege to run in some races that had unusual or spectacular finishes. In 2007, I had the opportunity to visit South Bend, Indiana, and run the Sunburst Marathon. That race started in downtown South Bend and finished on the fifty-yard line inside Notre Dame Stadium, allowing participants the thrill of running onto the field through the same tunnel used by the Irish football team. Race organizers even piped in the Notre Dame fight song as we ran through the tunnel. Although I am not a huge Notre Dame fan, I love college football, so this was special being able to run onto the historic field. After finishing, I watched one runner approach the field wearing a Notre Dame helmet. Evidently, his girlfriend handed it to him right before he approached the stadium.

My second overall marathon was the Grandfather Mountain Marathon run in Boone, North Carolina. This marathon began at Appalachian State University's Kidd Brewer Stadium at 6:30 a.m. and began at an elevation of 3,333 feet. The race involved a grueling climb to an elevation of 4,279 feet where it ended near the top of Grandfather Mountain in Linville, North Carolina. The course was heavily mountainous and very scenic as it wound through the Blue Ridge Mountains. Runners ran predominately on asphalt, with only three miles of the course on gravel. The race finished at McRae Meadows during the Highland Games, the second-largest highland game in the world, in front of over five thousand spectators.

After a race with my wife Sarah, my mother and father-in-law
Mary and Jim Lindsay, and my grandfather, Steger Preston.

Grandfather Mountain, my second overall marathon and first sub-three.

One of my favorite marathons was in the Nevada race at the Running from an Angel Marathon. This race had a spectacular finish, start, and in-between. Located entirely within Lake Mead National Recreation Area, the run started at Boulder Beach and led you onto the paved River Mountain Loop Trail. The January desert temperatures and views of Lake Mead made this run one of the most beautiful places I got to visit. It had plenty of hills, but being able to see the crystal clear Lake Mead blue along with the clear blue sky made every bit of this race enjoyable.

10

GOING INTERNATIONAL

For the remainder of 2015, I revisited five states and enjoyed seeing new sights. As the year ended, I started to think about a new goal: running a marathon on all seven continents. I had read a lot of comments from other runners about various races around the world. As someone who loves history, I was attracted to the Rome, Italy marathon. So in April of 2016, I took a long flight to Europe. The trip I chose was provided by a marathon tour group. I have found that this method of international travel is really the best way to go.

While in Rome, I got to tour several beautiful huge churches and visit well-known fountains. According to our tour guide, Rome has two hundred eighty fountains and more than nine hundred churches. Nearly €700,000 ($833,371.00) worth of coins is tossed into Rome's Trevi Fountain each year. The proceeds are donated to Caritas to help those in need.

As we toured, a highlight for me included visiting the Colosseum and the Roman Forum. I took a lot of notes from our wonderful tour guide as we spent close to three hours around and inside the Colosseum. Some interesting things I learned:

- Made from stone and concrete, this magnificent monument was built with the manpower of tens of thousands of slaves.
- The Colosseum is the largest amphitheater in the world! Oval in shape, it measures 189 meters long, 156 meters wide, and 50 meters high (about the height of a twelve-

story building). This ancient sporting arena could easily fit a modern-day football pitch inside!

- This brilliant building had eighty entrances and could seat approximately fifty thousand spectators who would come to watch sporting events and games. These events included gladiatorial combats, wild animal hunts, and, believe it or not, ship naval battles!
- Free for all! At the Colosseum's major events—often those organized and paid for by the emperors themselves—there was no entry fee. And free food was sometimes served too.
- The events at the Colosseum were seriously brutal.
- The first games ever to be held were in 80 AD, and they ran for one hundred days straight. Games continued to be held for centuries to come—gladiatorial games until the fifth century and animal hunts until the sixth century.
- To protect the spectators from the blistering sun and heat of ancient Rome, there was the *velarium*, an awning that could be pulled over the top of the seating area to provide shade.
- Below the Colosseum were numerous rooms and underground passages. Here is where the animals and gladiators were kept. There were also thirty-six trapdoors in the arena for special effects.
- Two-thirds of the Colosseum has been destroyed over time; mostly the result of vandalism, earthquakes, and fires.

There had been major terrorism in Paris the week before, so security was extremely high. One girl in our tour group tried to take a picture of the armed security outside the Colosseum and that made them angry, and she was scolded.

Race day was here, and I woke up feeling great. I was in a nice hotel about two miles from the start. After giving myself plenty of time, I walked to the Colosseum about ninety minutes before the start. With over twenty thousand participants, I knew it would take some time to get situated in the proper running corral. Sometimes the waiting is the hardest part of the race because as a runner, you are excited and ready to run.

Finally, the Italian anthem was sung, the wheelchairs and faster runners were released, and it was our turn. The course was a nice tour of Rome, including some of the nontouristy areas. But one of the most exciting things was running up to the Vatican City where several runners had photo ops with St. Peter's Square in the background. We also enjoyed passing these other famous and spectacular monuments and sites: Piazza di Spagna and the Spanish Steps, the Trevi Fountain, the Pantheon, Piazza Venezia, and Piazza del Popolo.

There were runners from all over the world, but mostly from Europe. Everyone's bib had their name and country flag, so you could see where they were from. I enjoyed listening to all the languages spoken on the course, and several people cheered for me as I ran by—"Go, Robert, go!"

Running on cobblestone was not easy, and with over twenty thousand runners, I paid close attention to my footwork. I had read in years past that when it rains, the cobblestone is almost like ice and very slippery. Fortunately, we did not have any rain. The weather was perfect at the start, but it got progressively warmer as the race continued. There were a lot of cobblestones in the last few miles, but there were hundreds of spectators and tourists at the Piazza Navona and the Piazza del Popolo cheering us on.

After enduring a tough uphill in a tunnel, the last kilometer was pretty much downhill, and I felt rather good. Still, I had to be careful on those last cobblestones before crossing the finish with the Colosseum in the distance. Halfway through the race, I was on my way to a sub-three-hour race, but the heat got to me, and I finished in three hours and eleven minutes. I came in 596th and was the fourth American to cross the finish line.

One of 7.7 Billion

While I was in line waiting for the Rome Marathon to start, I remember several sounds around me. First was the announcer making comments in Italian. I really did not understand any of it until the audible countdown from ten, and then I could tell we were getting closer to the start of the race. Listening to all the different languages around me made me think of just how many people there are in the world. According to Worldometers.info.com, there are currently 7.7 billion people in the world today. What an awesome feeling it is to know that, of all those people, God knows me and loves me. No matter where I go in the world, nothing can separate me from HIM and His love (Romans 8:38). And how great it was that He put this thought in my mind right before the race. Needless to say, I thought about this for the entire three hours and beyond.

11

Visiting the White Continent

I knew when I started thinking about the goal of running on all seven continents that one of them was Antarctica. After the Rome trip, I got serious about planning for Antarctica. It was by far the most expensive of all the trips but well worth it. Antarctica in the winter is not humanly approachable at minus fifty to eighty degrees Fahrenheit. The marathon I chose was scheduled in January, which was summer there with average temperatures in the twenties.

So in 2017, our marathon tour group flew into Punta Arenas, Chile, which is on the southern tip of South America. The group was comprised of fifty-eight people from all over the world. I really enjoyed getting to know my new friends.

When one flies to Antarctica, there are no guarantees. The weather can change on a dime, and you could be in the air, almost there, and yet be forced to turn around because the plane cannot land. Also when departing, one hopes to be picked up at the scheduled time without having to wait another day or two.

We were to be stationed in Punta Arenas for eight nights. The plan was to fly on the first opportunity of good weather. I was very anxious about this. I have read stories where a group was set to fly but waited in the airport for eleven hours because the weather suddenly turned bad in Antarctica. Another group was within twenty minutes of landing on Antarctica, and the plane had to turn back to Punta Arenas because the weather unexpectedly changed. Then another group was in the middle of running the marathon and had to be pulled off the course because the temperature was dropping dangerously low. They all eventually ran the marathon, but I did not want to have to go through that kind of ordeal.

When the pilot determined that it was safe to take the two-and-a-half-hour flight, all participants would have to be ready to go. After spending a few days in South America, the race director spoke with the pilot and announced we would be leaving bright and early the next morning. He also mentioned that if we were not in the lobby by a certain time, the bus to the airport would leave without us. That being stated, I did not get much sleep that night.

Our first chance to fly was at 3:00 a.m. on Tuesday. It was pushed back to 9:00 a.m., so we arrived at the airport at 7:00 a.m., and it was very relaxed. We were able to pass full-size water bottles through the Chilean version of the Transportation Security Administration. Or maybe liquids were not allowed, it was just the security agent being busy visiting with her coworker while our bags went through the scanner.

Our flight was only delayed by thirty minutes, and we were in the air before 10:00 a.m. It was exhilarating to think I was on a plane headed to Antarctica.

The flight to Antarctica was amazing! I am sure a big part of the fee was to pay the pilot. He was an expert, for which we were all thankful. As the runway drew near, I looked out the window and saw water, glaciers, and a small dirt-and-gravel path that was not very long. It was the only flight I have been on in which the passengers applauded as the plane came to a stop on the dirt path runway.

One feels like one is on the moon in Antarctica. It is surreal waking up to the most stunning sunrises and seeing the wildlife and icebergs. Television and even media just do not do these things justice.

I did some research after the trip and learned some interesting facts about Antarctica:

- Antarctica is the highest, driest, coldest, and windiest continent on earth.
- Antarctica covers 5.5 million square miles.

- The Antarctic ice sheet is the largest ice store on earth
  - o Area: 5.4 million square miles
  - o Mass: 7.2 million cubic miles
  - o Maximum depth: 15,669 feet
  - o Average depth: seven thousand feet
  - o Covers roughly 98 percent of Antarctica
  - o Contains 90 percent of the ice on earth
  - o Contains 70 percent of the world's fresh water

As we came off the plane, the wind was blowing extremely hard, and snow was going sideways. One of my fellow adventure seekers proclaimed, "We're not in Kansas anymore!" (referencing Dorothy of *Wizard of Oz*). We gathered our gear and hiked three miles to the base camp where we would be spending at least one night. With that hike, I was able to see some of where we would be running. My adrenaline was really pumping, and I was ready. The race director gave everyone thirty minutes to prepare once we got to the camp, and then he announced the race would start in five minutes. Of all fifty-eight people, I was the only one in shorts, but everything else was well covered.

Antarctica was different than what I expected. It was all black rock and dirt with patches of snow on the hillsides. It was not white and pristine, but I suppose it is summer in January, and most of the snow had melted. There was also a lot of moss and lichen. The temperatures were in the low thirties with a fifteen- to twenty-mile-per-hour steady wind that made it feel like the low twenties. I know it could have been a lot worse, so I was pleased.

The course was out and back six times. One turnaround was at the Chilean research base, and the other turnaround was at the Chinese research base, and our base camp was about the middle.

About eight miles into the race, I really started to take it all in. The beauty of a place that few people got to experience was exciting to behold. God had given me the gift of adventure as well as the ability to run, and I became so thankful for the opportunity. The race was exceedingly difficult with extremely rough terrain and heavy winds. But I enjoyed the entire experience and was fortunate enough to come in first with a time of four hours. I had read in the race reviews that most of the finishing times in previous years were at least an hour over a runner's average marathon time.

Race director congratulating me on the win.

Along the way, we runners saw several penguins. One of the female runners took a great video of a penguin trotting along beside her. I knew one of the hardest parts of the trip was still to come—spending the night in a tent in bitter, cold conditions. Before the day ended, several of us went on a little excursion to a nearby island that was home to one of the largest penguin colonies in the world. It was spectacular seeing an estimated one hundred twenty-eight thousand penguins!

It was time to get into the tent and try to sleep. I really cannot believe I camped in Antarctica. This was my first camping experience in a long time! Spending the night in the tent was an adventure. I am not a big fan of camping, and even though I had a great thermal sleeping bag, I was cold all night and did not sleep much. The race director did announce late that evening that the plane would be returning the next morning, and we would be departing to return to South America. That was extremely good news!

The camping experience brought back memories of my eleven years working for the Boy Scouts of America. I loved the people I worked with, recruiting boys and volunteers. I even loved fundraising. But one thing I did not like was camping. I remember exceptionally long nights trying to stay warm and tuning out the loud snoring going on throughout the campsite. It seemed like that was one of the requirements of being a scoutmaster—you must be able to snore!

One other interesting thing about the trip was the bathroom situation. At our orientation meeting, we were instructed how to use the porta potties. Pee in the white bucket, and poop in the black bucket lined with a plastic bag. We had to dump the pee in a big oil drum. The poop bag had to be tied and pushed into a poop tube. I know that is probably too much information, but it added more uniqueness to the trip.

The next morning, we toured the Chilean research base. The scientists must commit to two years, and they are allowed to bring their families. Consequently, they have a schoolhouse, and when one child has a birthday, the entire town attends. The woman who gave the tour grew up on the base, and she said it is a very tight-knit community. Our guide said the only "flower" in Antarctica is this lichen, and it takes one hundred years to grow!

We also visited a Russian Orthodox Church, which was built in 2004, and is the southernmost Russian Orthodox church in the world. The interior was gleaming with gold, and it was such a stark contrast to the cold, dark exterior. One of my fellow adventure seekers, Cheryl Hile, made this analogy which I love: "It was almost symbolic of my marathon experience. I ran in cold weather on top of black rocks, yet my spirit was beaming with gratitude for this amazing opportunity!"

Next, we boarded the plane and headed back to South America. The plane was heated though I was still cold from the long night in the tent. I did not warm up until I got back to the hotel and under the bed covers for an hour. Even though I was cold and tired, it was a great feeling of accomplishment.

One of the options for this trip was an opportunity to run a second marathon to be run along the ocean at Punta Arenas. It was several degrees warmer, but the wind was blowing almost as much as it was a few days ago. So after returning from Antarctica, sixteen runners were standing on the starting line getting ready for the second continent race in two days. I was not feeling great, having a sore throat, and really thought about sitting out the race, but I talked myself into it since I was already there. The race was another tough one, but I successfully completed it, finishing first in three hours and seventeen minutes.

12

Trip Down Under

During the summer of 2017, I ventured to Ayers Rock (also known as Uluru), Australia to run on my fifth continent at the Australian Outback Marathon. After another exceptionally long plane ride, I arrived safely and enjoyed the beautiful scenery over the next three days. The highlight of those three days was the opportunity to visit the Ayers Rock sunrise. As the sun came up, our marathon tour group was in the perfect position for viewing. We were positioned to see the sun's rays hit the rock formations directly as the sun came up, making them appear to change color; it was spectacular to see!

The night before the race, we had a mandatory opening ceremony and race briefing followed by a wonderful pasta party! The race organizers recognized the different countries represented, and there were over thirty.

We woke up quite early, and as expected, it was a chilly morning with the sun not even up yet. Buses picked us up from our hotel and took us to the start area, which offered beautiful views of the Field of Lights fiber optic light display at dawn, located right next to where we were gathered. Before starting the race, we were treated to a traditional performance by a local on the didgeridoo to start us off.

The course took us all along Yulara's hard-pack red earth fire trails that went all around the community. These trails are normally closed to the public but are opened solely for the racecourse that morning. Some of the red earth was easier to run on than others. Throughout the course, we would be kept abreast of our distance by kilometer markings, but of course, I had my watch set to miles.

After the first mile, we turned right onto what maps refer to as the Kali Circuit. This section of track was a little looser than the first mile, but still was not anything too tough to handle. We ran about 0.4 miles before turning a slight left onto a track that formed the back edge of the Uluru Camel Tours ranch, so we passed a few camels who were left back at the ranch before the regular sunrise tours had begun. We reached our first aid station as we made another turn further out into the outback desert.

Not long after, we could hear the humming of an aircraft in the skies above. A helicopter was positioned over the course, taking photos of runners as they ran under it, presumably with Uluru behind us. As you can see from the photo above, the end product showed some of the absolutely beautiful views we were treated to all around us. We continued along the fire trail, eventually reaching our first road crossing, Yulara Drive, the circular *main road* that encircles the resorts that make up the Voyages Hotels and Resorts community of Yulara.

We made our way around what seemed to be a water treatment facility for the area before running along the 1.5-mile long wide and flat Mala Road, where the sand seemed packed enough to be able to pick up some speed. Eventually, it became an actual paved road, and we made our way past some local homes, a solar park, and some industrial-looking facilities out in the middle of nowhere. We were sent back onto the red earth after seeing the only *major* cross street, and then followed a route far from civilization along the fire trails for the next three miles. The course stayed flat for the most part, but every so often, it would turn into single-track areas, where we would have to ascend a hill several feet, and then eventually down. The sand in these dunes was denser and was where most of the sand was able to get into my shoes. We never felt like we were alone out there either, as you could always see another runner in front of you or behind you. The aid stations were widely distributed, and one was very nice to see, out in the middle of the desert.

At around the 8.3-mile mark, we came off the sand once more and were able to run along the asphalt, following the side of the Lasseter Highway before turning left onto Harney Place. The corner of that turn apparently has some history, as Heidi Makinen, a previous winner of the race, had either forgotten to make the turn or went straight, going off course. Eventually, she found her way back on, and still won the half-marathon! The race organizers lovingly posted some signs on that corner and dubbed it Heidi's Corner after the folly that had happened. Eventually, we were led back onto the red earth (How could we not?) and would run through more of the same.

Ironically, I had later heard that the runner who came in second place had taken a wrong turn. He was way in front when it happened, and unfortunately for him, someone else came in first.

Overall, it was exceedingly difficult to run on red sand. The course was beautiful but relatively flat, with a few inclines and sand dunes. Considering the challenge of the course, I was pleased with my time of three hours and thirty minutes, which was good enough for sixth place.

The next day, I had a wonderful opportunity to visit a farm where injured animals were rehabilitated. I got to see a few kangaroos although they were very sleepy, probably because of the hot sun. I was really expecting to see more kangaroos on my trip but did not. It is interesting that as an American, I think of kangaroos as cute and fun animals. The Australians do not exactly see it that way. A couple I had dinner with one night said that there are way too many and they ran out in front of cars and caused all kinds of trouble. They told me that kangaroos account for over 80 percent of animal collisions and can cause severe damage to both the car and the animal. The chance of an accident is so high that most rental car insurance policies will not cover you if you travel between dusk and dawn in the outback.

And incredibly, there are more kangaroos in Australia than there are Australian people. According to NationalGeorgraphic.com, Australia is home to twenty-five million people and an estimated fifty million kangaroos, which some Aussies call *plague proportions*.

On the day I was to return home, I took a shuttle from the hotel to the airport. I was the only American on the small bus of eight people. One of the men asked me where I was from, and I told him I live in the southern United States in Tennessee. He responded with, "Oh yeah, that's where they drink whiskey, and everyone has a gun."

13

VISITING AFRICA AND WALKING WITH THE LIONS

In July of 2018, I decided to go to South Africa for my sixth continent. The race I applied for was the Victoria Falls Marathon, located in Southern Africa on the Zambezi River at the border between Zambia and Zimbabwe. The falls is one of the Seven Natural Wonders of the World and were spectacular to see. Can you name the other six? The falls joined the Great Barrier Reef, Grand Canyon, the Aurora Borealis, the Paricutin Volcano, the Harbor of Rio de Janeiro, and Mount Everest. I have been to several places near the Grand Canyon but never got to see it so that is on my list of places I would like to go, along with Mount Everest.

During my time there, I got to take a helicopter ride and see the falls from above. I am not big on heights but flying above the falls was incredible and breathtaking! It is the largest waterfall on the planet, one and a half times wider than Niagara Falls and twice as high. According to Victoriafalls.net, at its highest point, in March/April, it is estimated that five hundred million liters of water per minute flow over Victoria Falls.

I love animals, and during my ten days in Africa, I got to see all kinds, even in my hotel! Our group got to take a one-day safari. The first part of the tour was via boat, and we saw several interesting animals like crocodiles. After lunch, we boarded a Jeep and drove through a wildlife preserve. There were hundreds of elephants, and they came right up to the vehicle. We also saw giraffes, zebras, and lions, among other animals. It was truly a great day.

My hotel was a fun and entertaining place to stay. Every afternoon around four thirty, dozens of monkeys could be seen everywhere. One day, I even saw one walking up the hallway near my room. As one can see from the out-of-focus photo, I was a little startled when I rounded the corner and saw a monkey headed toward me. One afternoon, I placed a cracker outside my door on the balcony. It took about twenty minutes for a monkey to jump off the tree onto my balcony to enjoy the cracker.

When I arrived at the beginning of the week, participants were all given instructions to keep their balcony doors latched at all times. I listened and obeyed orders, but unfortunately, one of the runners did not. A baboon got in his room, completely messed it up, and even took his marathon medal.

On another day, I had the opportunity to ride an elephant which I had not done in years. Straddled on a huge animal for almost an hour, most everyone in our group had sore legs after we got off. On the final day before the race, we got to *walk with the lions*. This experience was a rush of adrenaline and will always stand out as a great memory.

After a very memorable week, it was finally time for the race. Typically, when traveling with a group, the race is at the end of the trip. I would prefer to race first and then enjoy the sightseeing and other activities later. I was ready to run! The race scenery was spectacular. The first part of the race had runners going across a bridge near the falls. It was a sunny, clear day, so it felt particularly good to run past the wet falls for a few minutes.

Overall, it was an extremely rewarding race. The marathon, half-marathon, 5K, and the concurrent Zambezi Man Challenge, were well conducted. There were over two thousand participants in all events, about four hundred fifty in the marathon. Even though the race was well-organized, it was run in conjunction with the half-marathon and a *fun run*. As we got several miles into the race, we encountered what seemed like hundreds of people on the road, and that made running a little more difficult.

We had a good number of water stops, but what made it somewhat difficult was how the water was handed out. It was in small, sealed plastic bags which were hard to open and made drinking a little challenging until I got used to it, five or six miles into the race.

Some hills made this more difficult than many races, but the view of Victoria Falls from the bridge was exhilarating. Running along the river kept the heat down and the views great. I saw a herd of impala crossing my path at 13K into the race. There was good support at the water stops, cheering in the residential areas, and just enough runners to know you were safe. The local people were very friendly and glad to have tourists in town.

Another thing that made this race unusual was the group of armed men at each mile. These men were stationed there in case a wild animal decided to run out on the course. After the race, I heard that they had to fire twice during the race to scare the elephants from blocking the path.

The last mile of the race was extremely difficult because we had to run on the dirt shoulder of a highway with participants who had completed the half-marathon, walking in the other direction. I finished in a little over three hours and was pleased to cross the finish line.

14

GOING TO JAPAN AND RUNNING WITH A TORN MENISCUS

Similar to nearing the completion of the fifty-state goal, the closer I got to the seven-continent goal, the more excited I got, and the more I wanted to achieve it. Number seven would be Asia, and I chose to visit Osaka, Japan in October of 2018.

I have been extremely blessed and fortunate over the years not to have encountered major injuries. Unfortunately, in September, about four weeks before the race, my left knee started to ache more than usual. It especially hurt when I would twist it or even flip over in bed from one side to the other. During the run, it did not really seem to aggravate it, but about an hour after the run, it would hurt. Also, getting up after sitting was not a good thing.

A friend of mine, who works as a chiropractor, examined it and told me he thought it was probably a torn meniscus. That was not really what I wanted to hear, and just weeks before the race, I was determined to get there.

Sitting on the airplane for almost fifteen hours did not help matters, but I tried to get up and move around as much as possible. I landed safely in Tokyo and then flew to Osaka. The people in Japan were extremely friendly, though very few spoke English. The language barrier made things a little challenging, especially returning to the hotel after I got out to sightsee. After a few taxi rides, I learned to take a picture of my hotel to show the taxi driver because the word *Marriott* meant nothing to him.

Osaka is the third largest cosmopolitan city in Japan known for its varied and magnificent food, vast underground shopping malls, and extremely friendly and outgoing people. With a population of 2.7 million, Osaka is the capital of the Kansai region, and the city is often called the Manchester of Japan.

During the week, I tried to stretch and even run some just to stay loose. My knee continued to bother me, and I simply accepted the fact that I was just going to have to persevere through any pain. When it was time for race day, I was excited but knew it might be a long day. Not wanting to take a chance, I reserved a taxi to take me to the race almost three hours before the start. It gave me plenty of time to get ready. I was hoping and praying that my knee would make it for the 26.2-mile race.

Getting ready one hour before the race.

The route was flat with a good-sized bridge that we had to go up and down twice. The Osaka Yodo River Marathon is just a long route that goes back and forth in the same area twice. Some might say that it was a very boring route, but I loved seeing a different part of Japan. We ran through a baseball park where several Japanese children were playing. They were so friendly and cheered as we went by. As the race went on, the sun came out, and it got a little warm. A few times, I wanted to stop, but I was afraid that if I did, my knee might start really hurting, so I kept going. As I got within one mile of the finish, I started to take it all in and realize that I was about to accomplish my goal of running a marathon on all seven continents. Despite the problem with my knee, I actually ran a decent race and enjoyed it. However, after the race was a different story!

Angel in Japan

After I crossed the finish line, I got something to drink and then found a place to sit down. According to the published race statistics, there were around six thousand participants in the race but less than five Americans. As I started to stand up, the pain in my knee was strong. We were probably at least two miles from the train station, and I really did not know where to find a taxi. My hotel was ten miles away. As I sat back down to gather my thoughts, a young man approached me and asked how I was doing (in English!). He had evidently just finished the race and saw me sitting there. I bet I did not look too good. I told him that my knee was hurting, and I did not know where to go to get a taxi. He was so kind and offered to help me. He said that he was from the United States but living in Japan and teaching English in one of the schools. We walked up the hill, onto a road, and then probably for another mile until he was able to get a taxi for me. I was so appreciative that my new friend went completely out of his way to help me. The next week, I looked up the race results and found my name, but his name was nowhere to be found. I believe he may have been an angel sent to help me.

"For He orders his angels to protect you wherever you go. They will steady you with their hands to keep you from stumbling" (Psalm 91:11–12 Living Bible). The writer of this psalm is recognizing God's ability to send down help to His creations through angelic means. The faithful are under the constant care and guidance of angels.

Returning home

The plane ride home from Japan was tough; sitting for several hours only made my knee hurt more. I was pleased that my goal of finishing the seven continents was complete but concerned about continuing to run. For the next few months, I tried to take it easier and lighten up on my mileage. Like I experienced preparing for the Japan marathon, my morning runs never seemed to hurt too badly but after sitting down at work, getting up was painful. I finally went to my doctor, a wonderful Christian man, who has always given me the best care and advice. Even more importantly, he prays for and with his patients.

After an MRI revealed what I feared, a torn meniscus, I scheduled a plasma injection. After undergoing this procedure, I would highly recommend it for anyone having knee pain. It helped me along with solid advice I received from an orthopedic surgeon, also an avid runner. I had considered statements from other runners about undergoing a *scope* or knee arthroscopy, and I had contemplated having the procedure. I also found that I had a condition called bony edema, or a bone bruise. Since the orthopedic doctor I consulted resided out of town, we communicated through his website blog, and these were his comments:

> Well…the risk of developing osteoarthritis (OA) does increase when you tear the meniscus itself. Having surgery to remove the torn piece does not alter that risk. It may in fact increase the risk of OA. If you have bone edema, then the bone is upset due to the increase in pressure or force it is subject to because of the tear. Running is often well tolerated in knees with these degenerative tears in the posterior horn. But it may take up to one year for the knee joint to settle down.

I found that, that was good advice. It was essentially *spot on* because it took nearly a year before I was able to run my normal schedule again. I stayed in shape by riding the bike and running in the pool at the local YMCA. I am now enjoying training, hopefully getting ready to start participating in marathons again. I do not know what the future holds, but I look forward to the next adventure.

15

COURAGE, CONFIDENCE, AND CRITICISM

I am very blessed to have a wonderful job as president of the Athens Chamber of Commerce. My success in running marathons has given me courage and confidence in my job. In return, the job has benefited me in running.

I have spent the better part of my life working for nonprofits. After eleven years as a district executive with the Boy Scouts of America, I accepted a position in 2004 as the president of the Monroe Chamber of Commerce, which is in the neighboring county. While with the Monroe Chamber, I started an event in which we brought in a guest speaker to motivate and entertain those in attendance. It was also to raise money to help benefit our community.

After two years with the Monroe County Chamber, I interviewed and was offered the same position in Athens. I genuinely love what I do by being able to help people and being involved with so many wonderful projects. I have also been blessed to work with some wonderful Christian ladies who I have hired, and they have all made work very enjoyable.

Transitioning to Athens, I brought the speaker event with me. In fourteen years, we have had some incredible motivational speakers including the following:

- 2007—Steve Spurrier
- 2008—Bruce Pearl

- 2009—Pete Rose
- 2010—Kirk Cameron
- 2011—Lou Ferrigno
- 2012—Phil Fulmer, Al Wilson, and Peerless Price
- 2013—Nick Saban
- 2014—Herschel Walker
- 2015—Peyton Manning
- 2016—Tim Tebow
- 2017—Amy Grant
- 2018—Bo Jackson
- 2019—President George W. Bush
- 2020—Jack Nicklaus

I have been able to take some motivational truth from each one which has ultimately benefited my running. Being just south of the University of Tennessee, bringing Alabama's football coach, Nick Saban, to Athens was an adventure. As I have mentioned before, Coach Saban was wonderful and due to his visit, I became a big fan of his! The adventure part of it started about five months before the event. I became the most hated man in Tennessee. I began receiving hundreds of ugly, threatening emails and phone calls from upset Vols fans. One example included from Rocky Top for Life:

> This is the ultimate disrespect to the University of Tennessee and all Vols fans, and it amounts to kicking us when we're down. It is the college sports equivalent of scheduling a Nazi to speak in Israel. I hope your power fails, your catering is illness-laden and that the backlash boycott sets Athens businesses back 25 years.

Another comment read, "I think Athens should be used as target practice for the United States Air Force. Beatings are in order for the Chamber President who booked Saban."

About seven weeks before the event, I received a comment that shocked me the most: "Whoever is responsible for this should be dead."

Thanks to a wonderful plan and great security, the event went off without a problem. The event was a huge success and covered by eleven television stations, as well as ESPN.com, *Sports Illustrated*, *USA Today*, *GQ Magazine*, and multiple newspapers including *The Boston Herald*, *The Baltimore Sun*, *The Wall Street Journal*, *The Huntsville Times* as well as newspapers all over the state of Tennessee.

The perseverance I developed through running helped me overcome the criticism and make something incredibly positive out of a potentially negative situation. It is almost humorous that eight years later, some are still upset about my decision to bring Nick Saban to our community.

Six years later, President George W. Bush came to our event and was wonderful. Working with the Secret Service agents for months leading up to the event was fascinating and very impressive. Our first meeting with them was six months before the event. I was nervous and expected tough-looking men in suits and dark glasses. They were all wearing suits, but it was great that they were so friendly and genuinely wanted our event to be a success.

Sarah and I were privileged to be able to sit at the dinner table with President Bush along with our county mayor, my chairman, and his wife. We talked about my running, and he seemed extremely interested. A few weeks after the event, he sent us a handwritten letter along with a book we had discussed during dinner, *Born to Run*. Overall, he was exceptional and very personable.

16

Why It Is Made Possible

I have accomplished a lot with my running, and I am proud of what I've done. However, it really means nothing if I do not honor my Lord and Savior Jesus Christ and recognize that all of this was made possible because of Him. Through all my travels, I have seen an incredible beauty that God has created. Over and over, He has protected me in my travels. There were probably many times that I was not even aware of how close I came to an accident or injury. Traveling thousands of miles and spending hours and hours on airplanes, I have drawn closer to Him through books and audio recordings which He has put in my path. I have also had some wonderful conversations with people on planes as well as with fellow runners when we've shared our faith.

If you are a Christian runner, you probably have Philippians 4:13 NKJ memorized, "I can do all things through Christ who strengthens me." When I first started running, this verse meant a lot to me, and now it means even more. When Paul wrote this, he was in prison and Christ basically gave him the strength to persevere in tough conditions and do it with a joyful attitude. I know He also gives me strength to persevere to the finish line in a race, but He has also strengthened me with the courage to travel to another country that had severe terrorism the week before. He has strengthened me with the truth of His word to get through depression. He has strengthened me with encouragement to get through injuries and setbacks. He has strengthened me with the desire and determination to train hard even on days I do not feel like it.

God has given me the ability to dream big and to persevere through anything. It has not been easy, and sometimes difficult and frustrating, but I know the one thing that is constant: God is with me no matter what and will see me through everything. I think about Romans 8:28 NIV, "And we know that in all things God works for the good of those who love him, who have been called according to his purpose." Sometimes when things happen to us, we do not understand why, but I can promise you that God has a plan for me, and he has one for you too.

If you are reading this book and there is some goal or achievement that you have thought about (maybe running a marathon), I want to encourage you to dream big and to go for it! I had the privilege to meet Tim Tebow when he came to speak at our annual Chamber of Commerce event. He is a role model in many ways. He maintains that "regardless of whatever I do, I know what my purpose is: to make a difference in people's lives." That is what I want to do as well, and I sincerely hope this book makes a difference in your life.

ACKNOWLEDGMENTS

My wife and best friend, Sarah, who has supported me and been patient with my crazy lifestyle.

My parents, Frank and Elaine, who lovingly instilled wonderful values in me and have always been there for me and our entire family.

My parents, Frank and Elaine, and Mark after
Music City Marathon in Nashville.

My brother, Mark, who pushed me growing up to be my best. We had some battles in the driveway playing basketball. He would almost always win but consistently made me *drive left* (I was right-handed) and taught me not to quit and to work hard.

My sister-in-law, Laura Norris, who helped edit this book and kept encouraging me to write it.

My friend, Bob Avento, who was with me at the very beginning of my running journey and would do anything to help me. He is a physical therapist and has given me wonderful advice throughout this adventure.

ACHIEVEMENTS

- One hundred fifteen marathons completed
- Marathons in all fifty states
- Marathons on all seven continents
- Sixty marathon wins, including Antarctica and South America
- First-place finishes in forty-one different states
- Podium finishes in forty-nine different states
- Average time of two hours and fifty-six minutes in the fifty states
- Marathon PR of two hours and thirty-seven minutes in Louisville, Kentucky
- Half-marathon PR of one hour and fifteen minutes in Knoxville, Tennessee

I can be reached at rob@athenschamber.org or 423-836-1823. I would love to speak to your group or church.

—

TIMELINE

- November 2, 1997—First overall marathon in New York City
- April 19, 1999—First Boston Marathon with a time of 2:47 (257th place)
- April 17, 2000—Second Boston Marathon; time of 2:43 (220th place)
- November 11, 2000—First marathon victory in Chickamauga Marathon in Georgia; time of 2:40
- December 14, 2002—First sub 2:40 marathon in Huntsville; time of 2:39
- October 19, 2003—PR of 2:37 at Louisville, Kentucky
- October 29, 2006—Worst time for a marathon at Marine Corp; time of 4:20
- September 20, 2009—Maui Marathon in Hawaii: time of 3:11 (8th place); decision made to run all fifty
- 2010—Best year as a marathon runner with five wins, including four course records
- 2012—Nine marathons including eight podium finishes with three wins
- 2014—Most marathons during a year with eleven; first time running two marathons in two days
- April 10, 2016—Rome, Italy marathon; time of 3:11 (4th American overall)
- January 31, 2017—White Continent Marathon in Antarctica; time of 4:00 (1st place)
- July 29, 2017—Outback Marathon in Ayers Rock, Australia; time of 3:30 (6th place)

- July 1, 2018—Victoria Falls Marathon in South Africa; time of 3:30 (73rd place)
- November 4, 2018—Osaka, Japan marathon; time of 3:48 (with a torn meniscus)

CPSIA information can be obtained
at www.ICGtesting.com
Printed in the USA
LVHW070335310122
709781LV00008B/89